HOW

TO DO

IBO-ORI

(Reconnect With Your Spiritual Essence)

OLUSEGUN DARAMOLA

COPYRIGHT

All Right Reserved

DEDICATION

To Humanity.

CONTENTS

TABLE OF CONTENT

ACKNOWLEDGMENTS

Learn the most simplest way to reconnect with your spiritual essence in both TRADITIONAL & ESOTERIC way.

This e-book (HOW TO DO IBO-ORI) details step by step guide on how to feed & venerate ones ORÍ known as IBORI OR IBO-ORI on your own & by yourself. You are your own priest & Priestesses.

As a Babalawo, I recommend this great e-book guide for those who want to know how ancient African conscious ancestors were connecting with their spiritual essence with the uses of natural materials.

You will learn the meaning behind different material we use to venerate our individual Orí & what each stand for.

You will learn how to pay homages accordingly & how to chant Ifá on your Ori.

HOW TO DO IBO-ORI is a must read for every serious seekers of Ifá & Òrìsà Spirituality.

CHAPTER ONE

WHAT IS ORÍ?

Orí can be translated to the word HEAD in English language but Orí according to Ifá is beyond the physical head, all living entities not just humans have their own Ori. The physical Ori that house our eyes, nose and mouth is the physical representative of the original Ori within. Ori is most sacred altar of communication & interaction.

Orí is closely related to destiny or fate because every details of one's destiny is encoded in Ori. Before we arrive to the physical world, we all choose our Ori individually. No ori is created equally. If an individual choose a bad orí, life on earth would not be so palatable but with good Orí, a lot of things would be easy for such person. Orunmila have the power to readjust a bad head to something meaningful.

ORÍ can become Òrìsà as times goes on with the right expression of such persons on earth. All Òrì is a potential Òrìsà. That's what gave birth to the word ÒRÌSÀ.

ENI ORI SA DA

Those who are uniquely chosen. Your activities on earth at the moment will show if you are chosen or not. Keep doing good and stay on the positive side of history.

Ifá says:

Ìwo Òrìsà

Èmi Òrìsà

Òrìsà di méjì a d'ebora

D'ífá fún Orí tí ń t'òrun bò wáyé

Èrò gbogbo e pèjo e sin Orí l'óba

TRANSLATIONS:

You, deity

I, deity

Two deities become divine

1

Consulted Ifá for the godhead

When coming from heaven to earth

All mankind assemble and worship the godhead as king.

•HOLY ODÙ ÈJIOGBÈ

Everyone embodies sacred deity and not until one is awaken to the divinity within, every forms of external worship and veneration would just only be for fun… For anyone to truly practice the consciousness of a particular (or numerous) deities and Òrìsà, such person must first practice the consciousness of his or her own divinity.

Yorùbá:

Orí làá bo, k'átó bò Òrìsà.

Translations:

(We worship the godhead within, before worshipping the deities).

Our head is the first deity, our consciousness must be acknowledged and even worshipped as that would direct our path to the recognition of the various divinity.

The ancestors lay down as part of the ancient wisdom the guide to which we can all venerate our consciousness and commonly in traditional practices every now and again we worship our head to clear our path for a seamless journey in life.

(Emperor Alafia Adeoba (2021)

Every items used to venerate your ori have a symbolic meaning and have power to influence your Ori with its energy. You will use the Ase to speak life into your Ori.

- Ori can be venerated with many materials as long as you know the essence of that material and sometimes you do not have to always wait to have all the materials before venerating your Ori, you can present anything to your Ori even if it's just water. Water have life in it. Cool water can be offered to your Ori. Honour your Ori with words of adorations.

CHAPTER 2

HOW TO FEED YOUR ORÍ (TRADITIONALLY).

What Is Ori Feeding (Ibo-Ori)

Orí Bibo/ Ibori/ Ibo-Ori Or call it Ori Propitiation is an ancient way of connecting to one's co-creator known as one's spiritual essence, the original 'I" in every human-spirit (ènìyàn.) It is the spiritual challace that holds every living entities destiny. Each individual have its own specific orí, the veneration of one's Ori is a way cleansing one's destiny with the power of natural materials àṣẹ.

CAN YOU FEED YOUR ORÍ ANYTIME?

Ibori is best done in the evening, at a time when you will not have to leave the house again for any reason. You can do it early in the morning also when you know you will be home throughout the day. Make sure you are very undisturbed that day because immediately after your Ibo-Ori, you need to be reflecting about your life as you remain calm & silence with your destiny. Take a good shower before your Ibori starts. Make sure the room or environment the Ibori will take place is very clean.

Learn to chant these verses to use along with each of the items for your Orí veneration. Even if it's just one of it you can chant before you proceed to offer your Orí the items, it is good. You can do this after paying homages.

(1)

Otutu

Awo abe omi

Adifá fún olomo mimi

Òun jẹ ṣe ti ori ran laje yẹ

Lo dáfá sí

Won ni o kara nlẹ

Ẹbọ ni kó wa se

TRANSLATIONS

Coldness

The priest of underwater

Cast Ifá for olomo mimi

That he can deliver the message sent to him by Ori successfully

Was the purpose of Idafa

Was told to be up

Ẹbọ should be done

Odù Irosùn Òyèkú

As I offer this items to my Ori, as I do this Ibo-Ori, may I be able to be strengthen so that I can able to be useful on Planet Earth & deliver my main purpose on earth, Ori please do not allow me to come into this life unfulfilled.

(2)

Iwŏran Olokun

A bára le kokoko bí ori ota

Adíá fun Ori-apere

Omo atakara sola

Njé ìbí ori gbe l'owo,

Akara

Orí jé wón o ká mí món won,

Akara

Ìbí ori gbé n bi'mo,

Akara

Orí jé wón o kay mí món won,

Akara

Ìbí ori gbé n nire gbogbo,

Akara

Orí jé wón o ká mí món won

Akara.

TRANSLATION

Iwŏran Olokun.

Cast Ifá for Ori-Apere

Who became wealthy by selling bean cake.

Wherever Ori is wealthy let me be counted along

Beancake,

Let me be counted along.

Wherever Ori has many children,

Beancake

Let me be counted along

Wherever Ori has all the good things of life

Beancake

Let me be counted along

- **Odu Ìwòrì-Ogbè**

PERFORMING IBO-ORI

Get a cap, hat or a pure white fabric ro tie on your head during & after your Ori veneration. It is a way of respecting your physical head which is like your shrine because all items for feeding your Ori should touch it.

MATERIALS FOR IBO-ORI

Water (OMI)

Honey (OYIN)

1 Big Snail (ÌGBÍN)

Kolanut (OBI)

Bitterkola (ORÓGBÓ)

Salt (IYO)

Money ($1) (OWO)

White Pigeon (EYELE)

Catfish (EJA AARO; LIFE OR DRIED)

Alligator Pepper (ATAARE)

Get all or some of the above materials on a flat tray.

Go before the materials prepared for your Òrì and knee before it.

You have the ASE on your tongue already. Àṣẹ is the energetic power of command or so shall it be from Olódùmarè (The Source Of Creation) everyone have it on their tongue.

Bend and be picking each material one by one as you will be using it to chant iwúre on your own head. Make sure you are touching your head with each & dropping it back on the tray.

The next thing to do here is **IBA**

PAYING IBA (PAYING HOMAGES)

This is important, it's an ancient way of acknowledging first Olódùmarè (The Source Of Life) & other living entities, a way of calling them to come and assist you on this spiritual rite. You can chant it in English if you like.

Iba Olódùmarè Oba ajiki

Homage to the Creator, the King who we praise first

Iba Ogege, Oba ti ngb' aiye gun

Homage to Mother Earth, who sustains the Universal alignment of all things in nature

Iba Onile

Homage to the Spirit of the Earth

Iba Elawori

Homage to the Spirit of purity

Iba'se ila Oorun

Homage to the power of the East

Iba'se iwo Oorun

Homage to the power of the West

Iba'se Ariwa

Homage to the power of the North

Iba'se Guusu

Homage to the power of the South

Iba atiwo Orun

Homage to all things that live in the invisible realm

Iba Ori

Homage to the Spirit of Consciousness

Iba Ori inu

Homage to the Spirit of the Inner Self

Iba Iponri ti o wa l'Orun

Homage to the Spirit of the Higher Self who lives in the Invisible Realm of the Ancestors

Orun Ori nile, e oo jiyin, e oo jabo oun ti e ri

The Invisible Realm of the Ancestors is the permanent home of the Inner Self, it is there that the Inner Self accounts for what it has done during the Journey to Earth

Iba Orunmila, Eleri ipin ikin dudu atewo, oro to si gbogbo ona

Homage to the Spirit of Destiny, Witness to Creation, the averter of Death, the Power of the Word that opens all doors

Iba Awo Akoda

Homage to the Diviner named Akoda, the first student of Orunmila

Iba Awo Aseda

Homage to the Diviner named Aseda, the one who taught Ifa to the world

Iba Egúngún

Homage to the Ancestors, I give respect to the realm of the ancestors

Iba Awon Iya Wa, Eleye

Homage to our Mothers, Owners of Birds

Iba Esu Odara, Okunrin ori ita, ara Oke itase, ao fi ida re lale

Homage to the Divine Messenger of Transformation, the Man of the Crossroads, from the Hill of Creation, we will use your sword to touch the Earth

Iba gbogbo Orisa

Homage to all the Orisa

Iba gbogbo Irunmole

Homage to all the Irunmole

Ìbá baba

Iba yeye

Homage to my father and homage to my mother

Iba se Iba se, Iba se o!

Now proceed,

Use liquid material to pray first.

Water: (Take Some Of The Wanted To Rub Your Head)

Chant

May water flush away all my worries, may you take away all poverty from my life. May you bring to me all blessings.

Honey:

My head, may this honey give sweetness to my Ori, may I and my family never know sorrow. May I always be attracting blessings to myself the same way honey attract ants.

1 Big Snail.

My Ori, may you have peace all through your existence on earth. May your path be s0mooth.

Kolanut

May my Ori reject sickness, death, poverty and all sort of ajogún (negative forces).

Bitterkola

May I live long and enjoy the rest part of my life on earth. May I be blessed with sound health and never will me and my family be spending money on sickness at the hospital.

Salt

May joy find its way into my life. May I be happy always. May my spirit keep evolving. May my helpers always locate me.

Money

Everyone wakes up to look for wealth, may I never lack you in my life. May I have you in my hands not on my neck..not in debt.

White Pigeon

The pigeon brings in blessings from left and right…all corners of the earth, as I am using you to feed my Ori. May you go and bring blessings into my life. Fly to corners of the earth to bring me my destiny helpers.

Catfish

As fish uses their heads to clear their own path, so will my Òrì help clear my path from all obstacles.

Alligator Pepper

Alligator Pepper always have plenty children (seeds) in it, may all my blessing be surplus. May all the Àṣẹ on my ori be activated.

Now release the snail to a safe place & Release the white pigeon to fly away.

Take the rest items to a flowing river, forest near you & if you don't have non near you, you can discard the items in the trash but it is advisable they are discarded to a flowing river or forest far from your home.

CLOSE THE ORI VENERATION

Let the cap or hat, white fabric on your head be there for a while before you sleep. Take it off before you sleep. Avoid sexual activities this time till after 7 days. You will see how your life will start changing for good.

CHAPTER 3

HOW TO FEED YOUR ÒRÌ METAPHYSICALLY.

Meanwhile, beyond any material offerings to Orí (as traditionally practiced by our native ancestors), the consciousness of our 'personal divinity' alone is enough — to set things right for us in times of trouble and to also act as a mediator between ourselves and our creator… While most people devotionally put faith in things traditionally offered to atone and appraise the divinity, what actually brings about spiritual effect are the "WORDS" that we speak consciously… As human, we can't always have the right items everytime around us to offer the divine within, but we always have the right "WORDS" at all time.

Waking up in the morning with "WORDS" of praise and blessing towards our individual godhead & Resting in the night with "WORDS" of thanksgiving and peace towards our individual godhead — are the best devotional practice to explore—and— empower the consciousness of our godhead.

CHAPTER FOUR

ADDITIONAL INFORMATION ON ESE (LEGS) VENERATION

A lot of people do not know the sacredness attached to their legs, Ori is great but do not let us forget ese. It is equally good and necessary. This is an additional information on how to feed legs to direct our PATH aright.

Ifá says:

Ìwo tè

Èmi tè

Díá fún Baba olórí ire

Má l'ésè ire

Ifá jé kí n l'órí ire

Kí n sì l'ésè ire

Eyelé lese ire

TRANSLATIONS

You initiate

I initiate

Cast Ifá for Baba with good destiny

Without good legs

Ifá allow me have a good destiny

And good legs

The pigeon have good legs.

Odù Ìretè Méjì

Note:

You can have a good Orí but not a good leg, everything is important in ancient Yorùbá world, all part of the human body is so sacred that there is name for each. ESE, leg in Ifá is an important part of the body that stand as Òrìsà on its own.

Feeding of legs is an integral part of Ifá as a way to reorganize or redirect our legs to take us to the right places at the right time. This shows that people can have good destiny (Orí) but have bad legs. You can speak life into your legs through the words of Ifá. Talk to your legs to take you to whenever you want and not to allow you walk when the path is hungry. The PATH (Ona) is another Òrìsà. We do feed Ona also in some cases. What does all these mean esoterically? It means ènìyàn have the power to change and speak into existence whatever they want.

Water is an important material of feeding Legs, a cool land is always easy to step on, no one would love to step on a very hot land. The coolness of water is being used to command ones leg to from today be stepping on cool lands. Cool lands here means stress-less places, acceptance in good place. Being in a place at the right and best time.

If you always walk into trouble, don't be frightened. Your good destiny will lead you aright. You will be fine. Whenever your head is taking you to, may your leg lead you there.

To have a good destiny & a good leg, you have to put YOURSELF on the side of what you know is true which is your Odù ifa, then the Truth will takes your side, lending you what is noble, needful, and divine.

Legs not just of humans but animals walk a PATH, PATH is a child to the earth and so honour is being given to her also. You have the power to speak to PATH, so you don't walk aimlessly in life and you will be guided aright as you are walking around the world as a Sojourner on earth. You should give respect to the PATH. Kolanut, water, pigeon (eyele) are part of PATH.

CHAPTER 5

HOW TO FEED YOUR LEGS IN EASY WAY

Get Water, Kolanut & Pigeon

Water

Make sure you have a direct access to the earth, Pour water on the sand and remove your shoe, step on the earth with water on it and chant the above ifá verse. When you are done chanting it in either English or Yorùbá.

Continue with chant,

No one block water from its path, may no negative energies (Ajogún) be able to block my PATH. May my Ori direct me to places where I would be celebrated. Feel free to be creative with the prayer by adding whatever you want and felt within to it.

Kolanut

May the powerful of this Kolanut block off all the energy of death & dis-ease on my PATH.

Pigeon

Pigeon (EYELE) have a good leg, may I always have a good legs. Pigeon walks into prosperity and blessings, may I walk into prosperity and blessings all the days of my life. As I release this pigeon, may the energy of this pigeon brings me Ire Gbogbo.

Some people kill the pigeon and touch the blood with your middle finger, rub it on your left and right toes. You can either kill or release it. Either ways works. You have the choice.

For those that kill, it is cooked & eaten with family mostly.

Ire o.

ABOUT THE AUTHOR

Olusegun Daramola is an Envoy and diplomat, Representative of African Culture, Chairman at IFA Therapy Global Limited, Author, Philosopher, Custodian of Global Culture, Creator of the Light of IFA Podcast, Promoter of Cultural Diversity.

He's also the High Priest at IFA Therapy School, a sub-brand under IFA Therapy Global Limited, where we teach IFA to the modern world, we teach IFA and ORISA Spirituality to awaken humanity from deep sleep of deceit away from dogmas.

Made in the USA
Las Vegas, NV
11 March 2024

87019755R00015